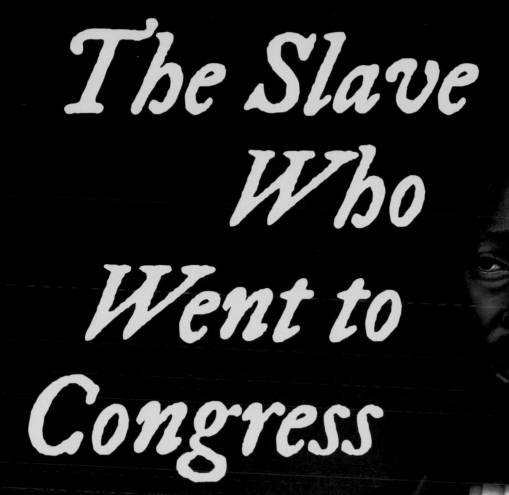

# The Slave Who Went to Congress

By Marti Rosner and Frye Gaillard

Illustrated by Jordana Haggard

NewSouth Books

To Mom and Dad. Education, indeed, is something no one can take from me. — Marti Rosner
To my family: Mom, Dad, Eliana, and Jaime. — Jordana Haggard
And to the countless unknown families broken by the history lived by Benjamin S. Turner. — Frye Gaillard

NewSouth Books
105 S. Court Street
Montgomery, AL 36104

Library of Congress Cataloging-in-Publication Data

Names: Gaillard, Frye, 1946– author. | Rosner, Marti, author. | Haggard, Jordana, illustrator.
Title: The slave who went to Congress / by Marti Rosner and Frye Gaillard ; illus. by Jordana Haggard.
Description: Montgomery : NewSouth Books, [2020] | Audience: Grades 4-6 | Audience: Ages 8-12 |
Summary: "In 1870 Benjamin Turner, who spent the first 40 years of his life as a slave, was elected to
the U.S. Congress. He was the first African American from Alabama to earn that distinction. In
a recreation of Turner's own words, based on speeches and other writings that Turner left behind,
co-authors Marti S. Rosner and Frye Gaillard have crafted the story of a remarkable man who
taught himself to read when he was young and began a lifetime quest for education and freedom.
As a candidate for Congress, and then as a member of the U.S. House of Representatives, Turner
rejected the idea of punishing his white neighbors who fought for the Confederacy—and thus for the
continuation of slavery—believing they had suffered enough. At the same time, he supported the right
to vote for former slaves, opposed a cotton tax that he thought was hurtful to small farmers, especially
blacks, supported racially mixed schools, and argued that land should be set aside for former slaves so
they could build a new life for themselves. In this bicentennial season for the state of Alabama, the
authors celebrate the life of a man who rejected bitterness even as he pursued his own dreams. His is a
story of determination and strength, the story of an American hero from the town of Selma, Alabama,
who worked to make the world a better place for people of all races and backgrounds"—Provided by
publisher.
Identifiers: LCCN 2019029924 | ISBN 9781588383563 (hardback)
Subjects: LCSH: Turner, Benjamin Sterling, 1825–1894. | African American politicians—Alabama—
Biography—Juvenile literature. | United States. Congress. House—Biography—Juvenile literature. |
Legislators—United States—Biography—Juvenile literature. | Slaves—Alabama—Biography—Juvenile
literature. | Alabama—Politics and government—19th century—Juvenile literature.
Classification: LCC E185.93.A3 G355 2020 | DDC 328.73/092 [B]—dc23
LC record available at https://lccn.loc.gov/2019029924

The Black Belt, defined by its dark, rich soil, stretches across central
Alabama. It was the heart of the cotton belt. It was and is a place of
great beauty, of extreme wealth and grinding poverty, of pain and joy.
Here we take our stand, listening to the past, looking to the future.

Book and jacket design
by Jordana Haggard
Printed by TWP America
in Malaysia

# Authors' Note

In this book for young readers, we have chosen to let Benjamin Sterling Turner, the slave who went to Congress, tell his own story. As a matter of historical record, his ideals and eloquent patterns of speech are preserved in two addresses he prepared for delivery in the U.S. House of Representatives. His white colleagues refused to allow him to speak, but his remarks in their entirety were printed in the *Congressional Globe* on May 30, 1872, and May 31, 1872. On April 21, 1871, Turner also testified in detail before the Southern Claims Commission about the losses he suffered, ironically, at the hands of Union troops who invaded Selma in April 1865. Turner's brother-in-law, Jackson Todd, prepared a brief contemporaneous document, "A Family Biography of Benjamin Sterling Turner," which can be found in the Selma Public Library, and which contains the colorful accounts of Turner's scrapes with authority when he was a young man. The authors are indebted also to the work of historian Alston Fitts, who has recounted Turner's story in multiple writings, including his book, *Selma: Queen City of the South*. Fitts made his extensive files on Turner available to Frye Gaillard for Gaillard's profile of Turner in the Winter 2012 issue of *Alabama Heritage* magazine. Turner's obituary in *The Weekly Times* of Selma can be found in the Selma library. In the October 15, 2008, issue of *The Nation*, historian Eric Foner wrote about "the courage of the forgotten black legislators of the Reconstruction era." The online *Encyclopedia of Alabama* contains a valuable summary of Turner's contribution to that history.

Forty long years I lived as a slave.

Forty years.

Mere property.

Thought of as nothing more than the mules, or horses, or furniture.

I've been told my life growing up in Selma, Alabama, was a privileged life, as there were others who suffered more than I.

But I would argue that no man is privileged when enslaved.

Even at the young age of five, I knew my place. Yet the desire, the yearning for an education lived in me as an illusion, an idea that would come alive on what I called the reading mornings.

On reading mornings, my curiosity would get the better of me as I crouched, hidden by the parlor door watching . . . listening to the magic of my owner, the widow Mrs. Turner, reading with her children. Reading mornings were priceless to me, as they opened the gift of possibilities.

I felt I'd found heaven when the children's nurse, a young slave girl, took me into her confidence. She had learned the alphabet from the mistress's children and taught me all she knew. I found books and newspapers from which to practice my reading and hid them, lest I be discovered. It would be a hard road if my efforts were found out.

Through sheer determination I carried on. It took years of stumbling over the printed word. The *New York Herald* and the *New York Tribune* became my friends. Listening became ever more important to me. Anytime there were political discussions which could affect my fate, I was there, the ever-efficient servant.

Listening.

Learning.

Once when I was nineteen, I was hired out to work at a steam mill and the overseer caught me with a spelling book. "If I ever catch you with a book in your hands again," he yelled, "I'll give you five hundred lashes on your bare back!" Alabama law forbade slaves to seek an education for fear that knowledge would increase their discontent. From the time of Nat Turner's Rebellion in 1831, white slave owners across the south were vigilant in the law's enforcement. Yet I, too, was vigilant in my dream of an education.

Nothing would stop me.

On another occasion that same year, the widow hired me out to a Mr. Winters with the task of arriving early to chop wood and create a fire to warm his house. One unfortunate morning I arrived late, infuriating Mr. Winters. When his son, a boy about my age, began to whip me, years of pent-up frustration and anger boiled up from within and spewed from me like hot lava.

I grabbed the whip and began lashing him with all my might. Knowing I had put myself in danger by raising my hand against this white boy, I ran home and hid. When the widow Mrs. Turner was confronted by Mr. Winters, she reminded him that his son had no right to touch me, and only she was entitled to punish me.

At the age of twenty, I was sold to pay off the widow's debt. It was to my benefit, being sold to Major W. H. Gee, the husband of Mrs. Turner's stepdaughter. He found me to be a valuable servant, placing me in charge of the family's businesses, the Gee House Hotel and a livery stable, where I took care of people's horses and carriages. I proved myself a responsible manager; efficient, honest, and trustworthy.

Upon the death of the Major and Mrs. Gee, the major's brother, Dr. James T. Gee, became my owner. Impressed by my business knowledge, he allowed me to manage his St. James Hotel, the largest in Selma. Also, I was given the privilege of hiring out my time to others and to continue operating the livery stable. Keeping a portion of the profits enabled me to save a considerable sum of money to someday buy my freedom.

When I had amassed $1,000, I asked the doctor, "Is this enough?" Laughing and shaking his head he replied, "You're worth much more than that! Even your four-year-old nephew can bring $400 on the open market." The sting from that encounter made me more determined to become a free man.

I cannot say the doctor was altogether unkind.

In 1857, he arranged and hosted a very fine wedding for me to marry a stunning slave woman I loved deeply. She had the most beautiful face I'd ever seen.

Independence was her name, but not her good fortune.

We lived happily together for a time, during which she bore us a son, Osceola. Shortly thereafter, a white man, noticing her natural beauty, bought her away from our precious family. I felt as if my heart had been ripped from within me. I could do nothing to stop it. I could only grieve her loss and raise our son.

Not long after, when the Civil War began, my thoughts once again turned to freedom. I pondered from which side I would be more likely to attain my dream. I was willing to support either in my quest to be free.

When the good doctor left for the war, he required that I go as his cook and body-servant. Our destination, Fort Morgan, was located on a nasty spit of sand which jutted out into Mobile Bay like a long jagged sword. It was a miserable existence—hot and humid, with armies of mosquitoes constantly attacking.

I begged permission to return to Selma, and Dr. Gee agreed, as his mother had asked for help in running the St. James Hotel. I was further allowed ownership of the livery stable and paid the doctor $50 a month for the privilege. I hired fellow slaves and paid them fairly so they, too, might prepare for when freedom would surely come.

Then on January 1, 1863, an amazing event took place. President Lincoln signed the Emancipation Proclamation declaring all slaves in Confederate states free. It was then I permitted myself a sense of hope, one of which I'd never dared speak.

Over the next two years, working daily with diligence and resolve, I operated the hotel and built my livery business. By the war's end, I had acquired $10,000 in goods and livestock, as well as hard cash. Managing the hotel and operating my livery stable placed me in contact with white and colored citizens alike. It seems I created a good impression, which would serve me well in the years to come.

When Union General James H. Wilson's army overtook Selma in April of 1865, I was reminded of the cost of freedom. Soldiers destroyed anything useful to the Confederates. As I stood in the doorway of my livery stable, the general charged up to me, looking down upon me from atop his horse, pistol pointing. Our eyes locked.

He shouted, "The Union needs these supplies and I'm here to be sure they get them!" With that, his soldiers commenced taking from me all I had worked so hard to gain.

My mules and horses.

My carriages and feed.

All gone.

Once again, bitterness and resentment were set aside in the name of freedom when Wilson called for colored volunteers to support emancipation. I gathered a regiment of men and became Captain of Co. A, 11th Alabama Volunteers. I saw little action, but much destruction, including several of my livery animals dead along the road. Once again, a grim reminder that freedom is not free.

With the surrender of the Confederate Army, I returned home to Selma and set about rebuilding my business. I now understood my emancipation meant more than being my own master.

It meant walking the road to a freedom where the rights of all former slaves would be a respected matter of law. For the time being, though the chains of slavery were unlocked, we remained tethered. We were free in the eyes of the law, but still enslaved by others' beliefs.

One steamy summer day, not long after the war had ended, a group of freed slaves were asked by the men who had once been their masters to work for pay. The freedmen, still raw with anger over their past enslavement, refused to do so. Fearing a riot, the former slave owners turned to me to persuade the men to return to work.

"Rethink your anger and remember our cause. Return to the fields. Be paid for your hard work and we can build a new future together so that all men can be proud," I implored.

They listened. Efforts toward Reconstruction would be laden with obstacles and in my heart I knew working together would be the better road.

In the years following the war, I used a portion of the money I had saved to start a school for colored children. It was also my honor to be appointed as Dallas County Tax Collector, and then to be elected to the Selma City Council, where I listened and learned much about politics.

In 1870, several leading citizens of Selma, both black and white, urged that I run for Congress. They had written a letter to a local newspaper expressing a high opinion of my abilities. It was humbling to be held in such regard. My reply explained my stance on the issues. My campaign slogan would be "Universal Suffrage, Universal Amnesty."

Some of my constituents were surprised by my opposing punishment for those white neighbors who fought valiantly for the Confederacy. But they, too, had suffered immeasurably, and I felt they should not be further punished. I favored the right to vote for all former slaves. I believed in mixed-race schools so every child could achieve an education. Of vital importance, the unreasonable tax on cotton must be refunded. Its burdens were unfair to colored farmers who had struggled longer and labored harder than any people in the world. I further urged the federal government to buy and set aside land for these families to purchase, upon which they could build new lives for themselves.

I was filled with hope. My opponent, Democrat Samuel J. Cummings, was a prominent white man. Although I was opposed by many whites, I had the support of the larger portion of the district, the freedmen. When the votes were counted, I had defeated Mr. Cummings soundly.

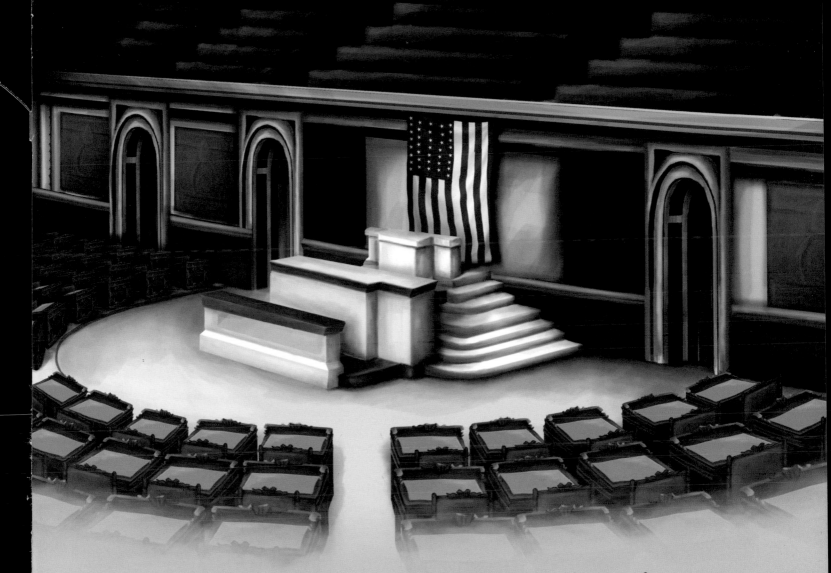

I thought back to those magical reading mornings, when my dreams of an education and freedom first took flight. Now I, Benjamin Sterling Turner, would take my seat as a free man in the halls of Congress—not only as a proud representative of the people of Alabama, but the first of my race to do so. I would do my best to bind the wounds of war and uphold the rights of all.

# Afterword

Elected in 1870, Benjamin Sterling Turner served only one term in Congress. His white colleagues refused to allow him to speak on the floor of the U.S. House of Representatives, but his eloquent speeches were published in the Appendices of the *Congressional Globe*. He offered a vision of racial harmony and progress that may have been ahead of its time. In one of his speeches he remarked, "I extend the olive branch of peace . . . let the past be forgotten and let us all, from every sun and every clime, of every hue and every shade, go to work peacefully to build up the shattered temples of this great and glorious Republic."

He lost his bid for reelection in 1872 when another black candidate split the African American vote, but he remained active in civic affairs and served as a delegate to the Republican Party's national convention in 1880.

Turner managed his own prosperous farm, hiring former slaves to work his land, and he paid for the education of the younger brothers of his second wife, Ella Todd Turner, whom he married as he took his seat in Congress.

He suffered a stroke shortly before his death in 1894.

In 1985, an interracial group of Selma citizens erected a graveside monument in his honor in the city's historic Live Oak Cemetery.